I'VE GOT FEET!

To Ellen, with thanks. –J.M.

For Matthew. –H.T.

Text copyright © 2017 Julie Murphy • Illustrations copyright © 2017 Hannah Tolson

Published in 2017 by Amicus Ink, an imprint of Amicus • P.O. Box 1329 • Mankato, MN 56002 • www.amicuspublishing.us

Library of Congress Cataloging-in-Publication Data

Names: Murphy, Julie, author. | Tolson, Hannah, illustrator.

Title: I've got feet! : fantastical feet of the animal world / by Julie Murphy; illustrated by Hannah Tolson.

Other titles: I have got feet!

Description: First edition. | Mankato, Minnesota : Amicus Ink, [2017] | Audience: Ages 3-8.

Identifiers: LCCN 2016052690 | ISBN 9781681521954

Subjects: LCSH: Foot--Juvenile literature. | Animals--Juvenile literature. | Anatomy--Juvenile literature.

Classification: LCC QL950.7 .M87 2017 | DDC 591.47/9--dc23

LC record available at https://lccn.loc.gov/2016052690

Editor: Rebecca Glaser

Designer: Tracy Taft-Myers

First edition 9 8 7 6 5 4 3 2 1 • Printed in China

I'VE GOT FEET!

FANTASTICAL FEET OF THE ANIMAL WORLD

BY JULIE MURPHY • ILLUSTRATED BY HANNAH TOLSON

amicus ink

Mankato, Minnesota

Animal feet can walk, run, and kick.
They can climb, jump, and dig.

Some feet swim. Some catch food.
What a lot of things animal feet can do!

I've got FAST feet!

My feet are as quick as
a car on the highway.

CHEETAH feet never slip. They have claws that grip the ground even better than soccer shoes.

I've got KICKING feet!

My back feet sure pack a punch. They help
me to avoid becoming a lion's next meal!

ZEBRA feet kick so hard they can break a lion's jaw!

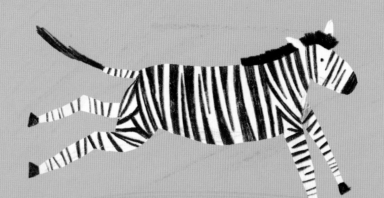

I've got WEBBED feet!

The skin between my toes helps me paddle in ponds.

DUCK feet are also good for waddling on the ground. They don't sink into squishy mud.

I've got STICKY feet!

My feet let me run straight up trees without slipping.

GECKO feet get their grip from thousands of tiny, bristly hairs on their toes.

I've.got SHARP feet!

My feet have pointy claws to grasp branches tight.

KOALA feet also have a toe that works like a thumb. Koalas need to hold on tight because they sleep up high!

I've got WARM feet!

My egg sits on my feet all winter long. If it rolled onto the icy ground, it would freeze.

EMPEROR PENGUIN feet have strong claws for gripping the slippery ice.

I've got HOPPING feet!

My long, flat feet are fantastic for bouncing through the Australian desert.

RED KANGAROO feet could jump about halfway across a school basketball court in a single bounce!

I've got BLUE feet!

I show them off by stepping high.

Male BLUE-FOOTED BOOBIES show off to attract females. Those with the bluest feet are chosen first.

I've got FLIPPERY feet!

My flipper feet make me a super swimmer.

SEA TURTLE flippers are fantastic in water, but they can be clumsy on land. That's why sea turtles only leave the water to lay eggs.

I've got STURDY feet!

My hooves hop over rocks without slipping or stumbling.

BIGHORN SHEEP feet are split for better balance, and they are rubbery underneath for great grip. They help the sheep climb steep cliff ledges.

I've got DEADLY feet!

My fierce feet have awesome claws that can catch all kinds of creatures for food.

GREAT HORNED OWL feet are so powerful they can even snatch up skunks, which are almost three times heavier than the owl!

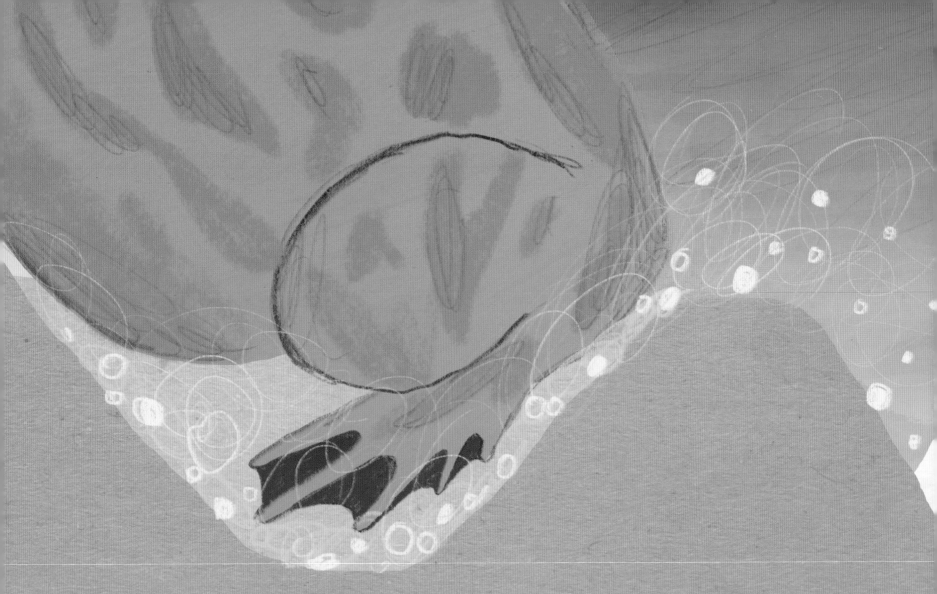

I've got DIGGING feet!

My back feet dig like shovels.

SPADEFOOT TOADS dig cool burrows in hot deserts.
They could not survive for long above ground in
such hot, dry places.

I've got HANDY feet!

Swish! I swing from tree to tree.
My feet are like hands.
I'm a chimpanzee!

Each CHIMPANZEE foot has a big toe that works like a thumb. It's like having four hands to travel through the trees in safety.

You've got feet too!
What can your feet do?

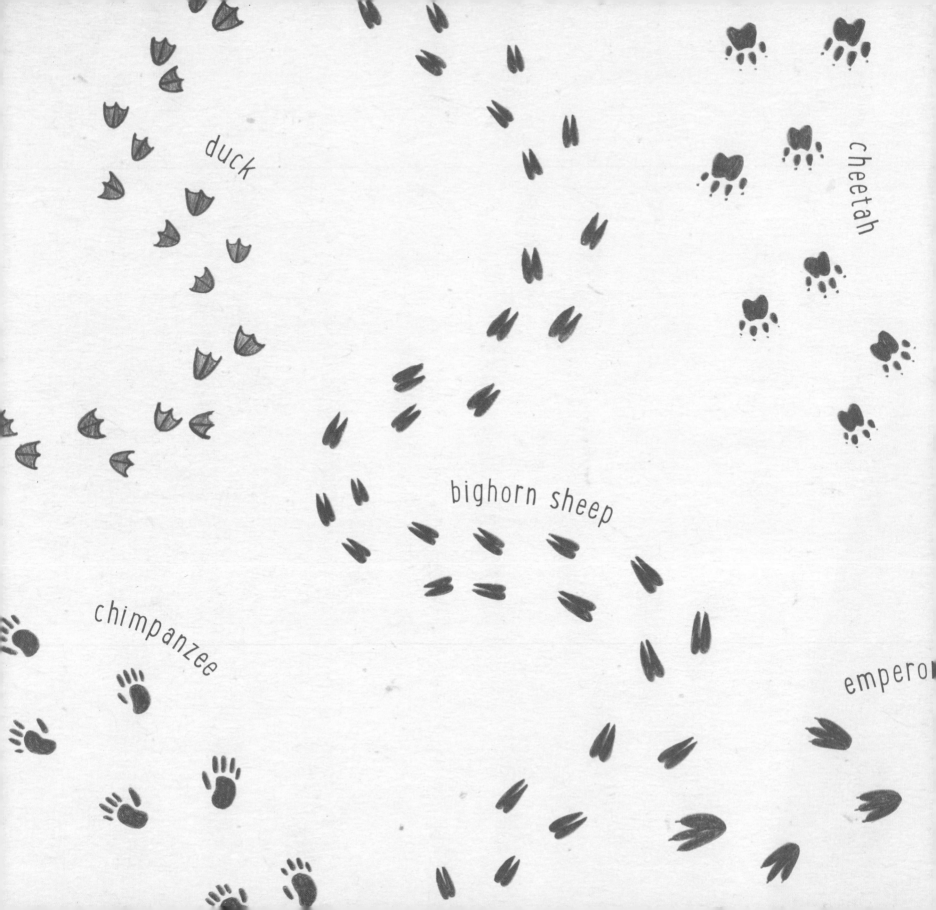

duck

cheetah

bighorn sheep

chimpanzee

emperor